# A FIGHTER'S
# *Journey*

THIS JOURNAL BELONGS TO:
_____

Copyright © 2021 by LaToya Dotson

All rights reserved. This book or any portion thereof may not be reproduced or used in any manner whatsoever without the express written permission of the publisher except for the use of brief quotations in a book review.

Limits of Liability and Disclaimer of Warranty

The author and publisher shall not be liable for your misuse of this material. This book is strictly for informational purposes. The purpose of this book is to educate and entertain. The author and publisher do not guarantee anyone following these techniques, suggestions, tips, ideas, or strategies will become successful. The author and publisher shall have neither liability nor responsibility to anyone with respect to any loss or damage caused, or alleged to be caused, directly or indirectly by the information contained in this book. Views expressed in this publication do not necessarily reflect the views of the publisher.

Cover Design: by Triv ilovedesignsbytriv@gmail.com

Printed in the United States of America
Keen Vision Publishing, LLC
www.publishwithKVP.com
ISBN: 978-1-955316-03-3

Writing has so many benefits. It allows us the space and opportunity to clear our minds, process our feelings, and keep record of our progress. During difficult seasons of our lives, writing is one of the best things we can do to help us press through.

I created this journal during one of my greatest battles to date, my fight against breast cancer. I used this journal to write out my thoughts. Some days, they were optimistic. On other days, I felt defeated. However, writing daily put me in constant reminder of God's faithfulness. Now that I have won my battle with breast cancer, I have those journal entries to look back on.

I don't know what you're facing, but I know that God is more than able to help you conquer and come out on the other side of this fight victoriously. Allow this journal to be your daily companion.

*LaToya Dotson*

*Today's Date:*

## HER PRAYERS

## Scripture

For truly I tell you, if you have faith the size of a mustard seed, you will tell this mountain, 'Move from here to there,' and it will move. Nothing will be impossible for you.

Matthew 17:20 (CSV)

## HER THOUGHTS

## HER APPLICATION

*Nothing is impossible.*

*Today's Date:*

## HER PRAYERS

## Scripture

The thief comes only to steal and kill and destroy; I came so that they would have life, and have it abundantly.

John 10:10 (NASV)

## HER THOUGHTS

## HER APPLICATION

*God gives life.*

*Today's Date:*

## HER PRAYERS

### Scripture

For all the promises of God in him are yea, and in him Amen, unto the glory of God by us.
II Corinthians 1:20 (KJV)

### HER THOUGHTS

### HER APPLICATION

*His promises are yes and amen.*

*Today's Date:*

## HER PRAYERS

### Scripture

The things impossible with men are possible with God.
Luke 18:27 (BLV)

## HER THOUGHTS

## HER APPLICATION

*Healing is possible.*

*Today's Date:*

## HER PRAYERS

### Scripture

Everything you ask for in prayer will be yours, if you only have faith.

Mark 11:24 (CEV)

## HER THOUGHTS

## HER APPLICATION

*Faith is key.*

*Today's Date:*

## HER PRAYERS

## Scripture

He also cured every disease and sickness.

Matthew 9:35 (GWT)

## HER THOUGHTS

## HER APPLICATION

*He cures all disease.*

*Today's Date:*

## HER PRAYERS

### Scripture

Worship the LORD with gladness; come before him with joyful songs.

Psalm 100:2 (ESV)

## HER THOUGHTS

## HER APPLICATION

*God is worthy of all your worship.*

*Today's Date:*

## HER PRAYERS

## Scripture

Behold, I will bring to it health and healing, and I will heal them and reveal to them abundance of prosperity and security.

Jeremiah 33:6 (ESV)

## HER THOUGHTS

## HER APPLICATION

*Prosperity and security will be revealed.*

*Today's Date:*

## HER PRAYERS

### Scripture

He sent his word and healed them.

Psalm 107:20 (AMP)

## HER THOUGHTS

## HER APPLICATION

*His word heals.*

Today's Date:

## HER PRAYERS

### Scripture

The LORD will strengthen him on his bed of illness.
Psalm 41:3 (NKJV)

## HER THOUGHTS

## HER APPLICATION

*He strengthens.*

*Every* DAY & IN EVERY WAY, *I'll get* BETTER *and* BETTER!

# A PRAYER FOR STRENGTH

Gracious Father,

You are the source of my energy when it feels like I have nothing left. You are the One I lean into. I will not attempt to defeat this battle in my own strength. You are the strength that keeps me going.

Because of You, I don't have to move this mountain on my own. Thank You for Your faithfulness towards me. Thank You for always answering me and meeting me right where I am.

Amen.

*Today's Date:*

## HER PRAYERS

### Scripture

Hear, my son (daughter), and accept my sayings, And the years of your life will be many.

Proverbs 4:10 (AMP)

## HER THOUGHTS

## HER APPLICATION

*God wants our years to be many.*

*Today's Date:*

## HER PRAYERS

### Scripture

For I will restore health to you
And I will heal your wounds.
Jeremiah 30:17 (AMP)

## HER THOUGHTS

## HER APPLICATION

*God restores.*

*Today's Date:*

## HER PRAYERS

*Scripture*

Everything is possible for one who believes.

Mark 9:23 (NIV)

## HER THOUGHTS

## HER APPLICATION

*Just believe.*

*Today's Date:*

## HER PRAYERS

### Scripture

He took our illnesses and bore our diseases.

Matthew 8:17 (ESV)

## HER THOUGHTS

## HER APPLICATION

*He bares our sicknesses.*

*Today's Date:*

## HER PRAYERS

### Scripture

Do not be afraid or discouraged, for the LORD your God is with you wherever you go.

Joshua 1:9 (CSV)

## HER THOUGHTS

## HER APPLICATION

*God is with you always.*

*Today's Date:*

## HER PRAYERS

## Scripture

Your word is a lamp to my feet,
And a light to my path.

Psalm 119:105 (NIV)

## HER THOUGHTS

## HER APPLICATION

*He will guide you through it.*

*Today's Date:*

## HER PRAYERS

### Scripture

Be strong and of a good courage, fear not, nor be afraid of them: for the LORD thy God, he it is that doth go with thee; he will not fail thee, nor forsake thee.

Deuteronomy 31:6 (KJV)

## HER THOUGHTS

## HER APPLICATION

*God will never leave you.*

*Today's Date:*

## HER PRAYERS

### Scripture

Who of you by worrying can add a single hour to his life.
Matthew 6:27 (BSV)

## HER THOUGHTS

## HER APPLICATION

*Do not worry.*

*Today's Date:*

## HER PRAYERS

## Scripture

Don't worry about anything; instead, pray about everything. Tell God what you need, and thank him for all he has done.
Philippians 4:6 (NLV)

## HER THOUGHTS

## HER APPLICATION

*Pray about everything.*

*Today's Date:*

## HER PRAYERS

### Scripture

Cast all your anxiety on him because he cares for you.
1 Peter 5:7 (NIV)

## HER THOUGHTS

## HER APPLICATION

*God cares for you.*

BY HIS STRIPES

I AM

*healed!*

# A PRAYER FOR HEALTH

Lord,

Thank you for knowing me inside and out. My heart, mind, body and soul are all important to You. You care about every part of my being.
I know that You are a healer. Touch my body and drive out all sickness and disease. Cast out every spirit of infirmity and affliction. My hope and trust are in You. Your word will not return to you void.

Amen.

*Today's Date:*

## HER PRAYERS

### Scripture

But you, O LORD, are a shield about me, my glory, and the lifter of my head.

Psalms 3:3 (ESV)

## HER THOUGHTS

## HER APPLICATION

*He is the lifter of your head.*

*Today's Date:*

## HER PRAYERS

### Scripture

The righteous cry out, and the LORD hears them; he delivers them from all their troubles.

Psalms 34:15 (NIV)

## HER THOUGHTS

## HER APPLICATION

*God delivers.*

*Today's Date:*

## HER PRAYERS

### Scripture

I waited patiently for the LORD to help me, and he turned to me and heard my cry.
Psalms 40:1 (NLV)

## HER THOUGHTS

## HER APPLICATION

*God hears our cry.*

*Today's Date:*

## HER PRAYERS

## Scripture

Truly, truly, I say to you, whatever you ask of the Father in my name, he will give it to you.

John 16:23 (ESV)

## HER THOUGHTS

## HER APPLICATION

*Ask and receive.*

**Today's Date:**

## HER PRAYERS

### Scripture

Restore to me the joy of your salvation and grant me a willing spirit, to sustain me.

Psalm 51:12 (ESV)

### HER THOUGHTS

### HER APPLICATION

*God will restore your joy and sustain you.*

*Today's Date:*

## HER PRAYERS

### Scripture

To another faith by the same Spirit, to another gifts of healing by that one Spirit.
1 Corinthian 12:9 (NIV)

## HER THOUGHTS

## HER APPLICATION

*Command your healing!*

*Today's Date:*

## HER PRAYERS

### Scripture

Weeping may endure for a night, but joy comes in the morning.

Psalms 30:5 (KJV)

## HER THOUGHTS

## HER APPLICATION

*Joy will come in the morning.*

*Today's Date:*

## HER PRAYERS

### Scripture

He heals the brokenhearted and binds up their wounds.
Psalms 147:3 (NIV)

## HER THOUGHTS

## HER APPLICATION

*He heals.*

*Today's Date:*

## HER PRAYERS

## Scripture

For we live by faith, not by sight.

2 Corinthians 5:7 (NIV)

## HER THOUGHTS

## HER APPLICATION

*Live by faith.*

*Today's Date:*

## HER PRAYERS

### Scripture

Now faith is the substance of things hoped for, the evidence of things not seen.

Hebrews 11:1 (KJV)

## HER THOUGHTS

## HER APPLICATION

*Faith is all you need.*

*My circumstance is*
# IMPROVING!

# A PRAYER FOR STRESS

Dear God,

I come to You overwhelmed by the opposition that stands before me. Allow Your peace to rush over me. I yield my heart to You. I surrender and welcome You to provide the clarity I need.

When my mind is in an uproar, help me to slow down, seek You, and hearken to Your voice. Thank You for being my portion in every circumstance. I put my trust in You.

Amen.

Today's Date:

## HER PRAYERS

### Scripture

For God has not given us a spirit of fear and timidity, but of power, love, and self-discipline.
2 Timothy 1:7 (NLV)

## HER THOUGHTS

## HER APPLICATION

*Fear is not of God.*

Today's Date:

## HER PRAYERS

### Scripture

They do not fear bad news; they confidently trust the LORD to care for them.

Psalm 112:7 (NLT)

## HER THOUGHTS

## HER APPLICATION

*Do not fear, trust God*

*Today's Date:*

## HER PRAYERS

### Scripture

He forgives all my sins and heals all my diseases.
Psalms 103:3 (NLT)

## HER THOUGHTS

## HER APPLICATION

*He heals and forgives.*

*Today's Date:*

## HER PRAYERS

### Scripture

Heal me, O Lord, and I shall be healed; save me, and I shall be saved, for you are my praise.
Jeremiah 17:14 (ESV)

## HER THOUGHTS

## HER APPLICATION

*Praise heals and saves.*

*Today's Date:*

## HER PRAYERS

### Scripture

The LORD is my portion, saith my soul; therefore will I hope in him.

Lamentations 3:24 (KJV)

## HER THOUGHTS

## HER APPLICATION

*Put your hope in the Lord.*

*Today's Date:*

## HER PRAYERS

### Scripture

Be joyful in hope, patient in affliction, faithful in prayer.
Romans 12:12 (NIV)

## HER THOUGHTS

## HER APPLICATION

*Be patient.*

*Today's Date:*

## HER PRAYERS

## Scripture

I waited patiently and expectantly for the Lord, and he inclined to me and heard my cry.

Psalms 40:1 (ESV)

## HER THOUGHTS

## HER APPLICATION

*Be expectant.*

*Today's Date:*

## HER PRAYERS

### Scripture

And let us not grow weary of doing good, for in due season we will reap, if we do not give up.

Galatians 6:9 (ESV)

## HER THOUGHTS

## HER APPLICATION

*Don't give up.*

*Today's Date:*

## HER PRAYERS

### Scripture

Now may the Lord of peace himself give you his peace at all times and in every situation. The Lord be with you all.
2 Thessalonians 3:16 (AMP)

## HER THOUGHTS

## HER APPLICATION

*He will give you peace at all times.*

*Today's Date:*

## HER PRAYERS

### Scripture

But thanks be to God! He gives us the victory through our Lord Jesus Christ.

1 Corinthians 15:57 (NIV)

## HER THOUGHTS

## HER APPLICATION

*Victory is in Christ Jesus.*

*I Will win*

# THIS FIGHT!

# A PRAYER FOR PATIENCE

Father,

I know that most things don't come quickly and there is a purpose for every process. However, waiting can be extremely hard. Please grant me the ability to be patient. Help me to have a broader perspective and see the bigger picture. Relieve my anxiety. Help me to have a positive attitude. I know that when You guide me in this aspect of my life, my heart and mind will be transformed. Help me to trust You completely.

Amen.

*Today's Date:*

## HER PRAYERS

### Scripture

He gives power to the weak and strength to the powerless (making you stronger.
Isaiah 40:29 (NLV)

## HER THOUGHTS

## HER APPLICATION

*He gives strength and power.*

*Today's Date:*

## HER PRAYERS

### Scripture

He drives out the enemy before you, giving the command, 'Destroy him!
Deuteronomy 33:27 (BSV)

## HER THOUGHTS

## HER APPLICATION

*God destroys the enemy.*

*Today's Date:*

## HER PRAYERS

### Scripture

The LORD is a refuge for the oppressed, a stronghold in times of trouble.

Psalms 9:9 (NIV)

## HER THOUGHTS

## HER APPLICATION

*The Lord is your refuge.*

*Today's Date:*

## HER PRAYERS

### Scripture

He who dwells in the shelter of the Most High will abide in the shadow of the Almighty.

Psalms 91:1-2 (ESV)

## HER THOUGHTS

## HER APPLICATION

*Abide in his shadow.*

*Today's Date:*

## HER PRAYERS

### Scripture

I want all of you to be free from worry.

I Corinthians 32 (CEV)

## HER THOUGHTS

## HER APPLICATION

*Cast your cares on him.*

*Today's Date:*

## HER PRAYERS

*Scripture*

Behold, we consider those blessed who remained steadfast. You have heard of the steadfastness of Job, and you have seen the purpose of the Lord, how the Lord is compassionate and merciful. James 5:11 (ESV)

## HER THOUGHTS

## HER APPLICATION

*Remain steadfast.*

*Today's Date:*

## HER PRAYERS

## Scripture

Blessed is the man who remains steadfast under trial, for when he has stood the test he will receive the crown of life, which God has promised to those who love him.

James 1:12 (ESV)

## HER THOUGHTS

## HER APPLICATION

*Pass the test.*

*Today's Date:*

## HER PRAYERS

### Scripture

For you have need of endurance, so that when you have done the will of God you may receive what is promised.

Hebrews 10:36 (ESV)

## HER THOUGHTS

## HER APPLICATION

*Your promise awaits you.*

*Today's Date:*

## HER PRAYERS

### Scripture

May the Lord direct your hearts to the love of God and to the steadfastness of Christ.
2 Thessalonians 3:5 (ESV)

## HER THOUGHTS

## HER APPLICATION

*God's love covers you.*

*Today's Date:*

## HER PRAYERS

## Scripture

Seek the Lord and his strength;
seek his presence continually!
1 Chronicles 16:11 (ESV)

## HER THOUGHTS

## HER APPLICATION

*Remain in His presence.*

# WHEN I AM
## *weak*
# HE IS
## *Strong!*

# A PRAYER FOR ENDURANCE

Mighty God,

I cannot make it through this battle alone. I have tried in my own strength and it didn't work. Give me the strength to keep going. Be the lifter of my head when weakness seems to overtake me. When I have nothing to give, remind me to lean closer into You. Give me the strength to endure. Remind me that the reward that awaits me is greater than the discomfort I may be facing. Help me to endure with great faith that You will give me the victory.

Amen.

**Today's Date:**

## HER PRAYERS

### Scripture

May you be strengthened with all power, according to his glorious might, for all endurance and patience with joy.

Colossians 1:11 (ESV)

## HER THOUGHTS

## HER APPLICATION

*Have patience and joy.*

*Today's Date:*

## HER PRAYERS

### Scripture

Let us hold fast the confession of our hope without wavering, for he who promised is faithful.
Hebrews 10:23 (ESV)

## HER THOUGHTS

## HER APPLICATION

*God is faithful.*

**Today's Date:**

## HER PRAYERS

### Scripture

Looking to Jesus, the founder and perfecter of our faith, who for the joy that was set before him endured the cross, despising the shame, and is seated at the right hand of the throne of God.

Hebrews 12:2 (ESV)

## HER THOUGHTS

## HER APPLICATION

*Look to Jesus.*

*Today's Date:*

## HER PRAYERS

*Scripture*

And whatever you ask in prayer, you will receive, if you have faith.

Matthew 21:22 (ESV)

## HER THOUGHTS

## HER APPLICATION

*Pray in faith!*

*Today's Date:*

## HER PRAYERS

### Scripture

And without faith it is impossible to please him, for whoever would draw near to God must believe that he exists and that he rewards those who seek him.

Hebrews 11:6 (ESV)

## HER THOUGHTS

## HER APPLICATION

*God rewards those who seek Him.*

*Today's Date:*

## HER PRAYERS

### Scripture

That your faith might not rest in the wisdom of men but in the power of God.
1 Corinthians 2:5 (ESV)

## HER THOUGHTS

## HER APPLICATION

*Put your faith in God, not man.*

*Today's Date:*

## HER PRAYERS

### Scripture

For everyone who has been born of God overcomes the world. And this is the victory that has overcome the world— our faith.

1 John 5:4 (ESV)

## HER THOUGHTS

## HER APPLICATION

*You shall overcome.*

*Today's Date:*

## HER PRAYERS

## Scripture

But in your hearts honor Christ the Lord as holy, always being prepared to make a defense to anyone who asks you for a reason for the hope that is in you; yet do it with gentleness and respect.

1 Peter 3:15 (ESV)

## HER THOUGHTS

## HER APPLICATION

*Declare that your hope is in Christ!*

**Today's Date:**

## HER PRAYERS

### Scripture

Fight the good fight of the faith. Take hold of the eternal life to which you were called and about which you made the good confession in the presence of many witnesses.

1 Timothy 6:12 (ESV)

## HER THOUGHTS

## HER APPLICATION

*Cast your cares on him.*

*Today's Date:*

## HER PRAYERS

*Scripture*

In all circumstances take up the shield of faith, with which you can extinguish all the flaming darts of the evil one.

Ephesians 6:16 (ESV)

## HER THOUGHTS

## HER APPLICATION

*Abide in his shadow.*

# GOD REFRESHES

*my soul.*

# A PRAYER FOR PEACE

Dear Lord,

I have been so full of anxiety and worry. Your word lets us know that we would have trouble in this world but You are our rescue. I am grateful that You have given us the gift of peace. You give peace to our minds and our hearts.

Grant me peace that surpasses all understanding. I receive it with an open heart and open arms.

Amen.

*Today's Date:*

## HER PRAYERS

### Scripture

The Lord your God is in your midst — a warrior bringing victory. He will create calm with his love; he will rejoice over you with singing.
Zephaniah 3:17 (ESV)

## HER THOUGHTS

## HER APPLICATION

*God rejoices over you with singing.*

*Today's Date:*

## HER PRAYERS

## Scripture

Know now then that the Lord your God is the only true God! He is the faithful God, who keeps the covenant and proves loyal to everyone who loves him and keeps his commands — even to the thousandth generation!

Deuteronomy 7:9 (ESV)

## HER THOUGHTS

## HER APPLICATION

*Your God is loyal to those who love Him.*

*Today's Date:*

## HER PRAYERS

### Scripture

I ask that you'll have the power to grasp love's width and length, height and depth, together with all believers.

Ephesians 3:18 (ESV)

## HER THOUGHTS

## HER APPLICATION

*God's love surrounds you.*

*Today's Date:*

## HER PRAYERS

### Scripture

Give thanks to the Lord because he is good, because his faithful love endures forever.

1 Chronicles 16:34 (ESV)

## HER THOUGHTS

## HER APPLICATION

*The Lord is good!*

*Today's Date:*

## HER PRAYERS

### Scripture

"Let them thank the Lord for his faithful love and his wondrous works for all people, because God satisfied the one who was parched with thirst, and he filled up the hungry with good things!"

Psalm 107:8-9 (ESV)

## HER THOUGHTS

## HER APPLICATION

*God will satisfy your every need.*

*Today's Date:*

## HER PRAYERS

### Scripture

He said: 'Lord God of Israel, there is no god like you in heaven or on the earth. You keep the covenant and show loyalty to your servants who walk before you with all their heart.

2 Chronicles 6:14 (ESV)

## HER THOUGHTS

## HER APPLICATION

*There is no God like our God!*

*Today's Date:*

## HER PRAYERS

## Scripture

"So what are we going to say about these things? If God is for us, who is against us? He didn't spare his own Son but gave him up for us all. Won't he also freely give us all things with him?"

Romans 8:31-32 (ESV)

## HER THOUGHTS

## HER APPLICATION

*God is for you!*

*Today's Date:*

## HER PRAYERS

## Scripture

Your faithful love is priceless, God! Humanity finds refuge in the shadow of your wings.
Psalm 36:7 (ESV)

## HER THOUGHTS

## HER APPLICATION

*Find refuge in His wings!*

*Today's Date:*

## HER PRAYERS

*Scripture*

But you, Lord, my Lord! — act on my behalf for the sake of your name; deliver me because your faithful love is so good.

Psalm 109:21 (ESV)

## HER THOUGHTS

## HER APPLICATION

*God's faithful love is so good!*

Today's Date:

## HER PRAYERS

### Scripture

This hope doesn't put us to shame, because the love of God has been poured out in our hearts through the Holy Spirit, who has been given to us.
Romans 5:5 (ESV)

## HER THOUGHTS

## HER APPLICATION

*Ask God to increase your faith!*

# MY GOD IS A *covenant keeping* GOD!

# A PRAYER FOR PROMISES

Most Gracious Father,

You are faithful in all that You do. Even when it seems that I can't trace You, You always follow through. When days get hard, help me to remember Your word. As I wait to see the manifestation of your promises, remind me that You are building my faith.

Although my situation seems grim, trouble doesn't last always and joy comes in the morning. Help me to hold tightly to Your promises when nothing else seems certain.

Amen.

*Today's Date:*

## HER PRAYERS

## *Scripture*

The mountains may shift, and the hills may be shaken, but my faithful love won't shift from you, and my covenant of peace won't be shaken,' says the Lord, the one who pities you.

Isaiah 54:10 (ESV)

## HER THOUGHTS

## HER APPLICATION

*God's love for you can't be shaken!*

*Today's Date:*

## HER PRAYERS

### Scripture

But you, my Lord, are a God of compassion and mercy; you are very patient and full of faithful love.

Psalm 86:15 (ESV)

## HER THOUGHTS

## HER APPLICATION

*Be reminded of God's faithful love for you!*

*Today's Date:*

## HER PRAYERS

## *Scripture*

May the God of hope fill you with all joy and peace in believing, so that by the power of the Holy Spirit you may abound in hope.

Romans 15:13 (ESV)

## HER THOUGHTS

## HER APPLICATION

*Allow His joy and peace to fill you!*

*Today's Date:*

## HER PRAYERS

### Scripture

Let us then with confidence draw near to the throne of grace, that we may receive mercy and find grace to help in time of need.

Hebrews 4:16 (ESV)

## HER THOUGHTS

## HER APPLICATION

*His mercy and grace is available to you.*

*Today's Date:*

## HER PRAYERS

## Scripture

But by the grace of God I am what I am, and his grace toward me was not in vain. On the contrary, I worked harder than any of them, though it was not I, but the grace of God that is with me.

1 Corinthians 15:10 (ESV)

## HER THOUGHTS

## HER APPLICATION

*God's grace is at work within you.*

*Today's Date:*

## HER PRAYERS

### Scripture

Taste and see that the LORD is good; blessed is the one who takes refuge in him.

Psalm 34:8 (ESV)

## HER THOUGHTS

## HER APPLICATION

*Take refuge in the Lord.*

*Today's Date:*

## HER PRAYERS

### Scripture

And Jesus said to him, "Go your way; your faith has made you well." And immediately he recovered his sight and followed him on the way.
Mark 10:52 (ESV)

## HER THOUGHTS

## HER APPLICATION

*Your faith will make all things concerning you well!*

Today's Date:

## HER PRAYERS

### Scripture

"Therefore I tell you, whatever you ask in prayer, believe that you have received it, and it will be yours."

Mark 11:24 (ESV)

## HER THOUGHTS

## HER APPLICATION

*Believe and you shall receive it!*

Today's Date:

## HER PRAYERS

### Scripture

So shall my word be that goes out from my mouth; it shall not return to me empty, but it shall accomplish that which I purpose, and shall succeed in the thing for which I sent it.
— Isaiah 55:11 (ESV)

## HER THOUGHTS

## HER APPLICATION

*God's word always prevails.*

*Today's Date:*

## HER PRAYERS

### Scripture

"God is in the midst of her; she shall not be moved; God will help her when morning dawns."

Psalm 46:5 (ESV)

## HER THOUGHTS

## HER APPLICATION

*You will not be moved!*

I FIND
SAFETY
*under His wings.*

# A PRAYER FOR FEAR

Heavenly Father,

I know I can be honest and tell you when I am afraid. You are my safe place. Remind me that You have not given me a spirit of fear. Help me to use power, love, and a sound mind to defeat everything I'm faced with.

You have a plan for my life. Your intentions for me are good. The power of Your love makes me fearless. With You on my side, it doesn't matter who or what is against me. I will end this battle victoriously.

Amen.

**Today's Date:**

## HER PRAYERS

## Scripture

So we can confidently say, "The Lord is my helper; I will not fear; what can man do to me?"
Hebrews 13:6 (ESV)

## HER THOUGHTS

## HER APPLICATION

*The Lord is your helper.*

Today's Date:

## HER PRAYERS

### Scripture

The Lord is my light and my salvation; whom shall I fear? The Lord is the stronghold of my life; of whom shall I be afraid?

Psalm 27:1 (ESV)

## HER THOUGHTS

## HER APPLICATION

*You have no reason to fear.*

*Today's Date:*

## HER PRAYERS

### Scripture

I praise you, for I am fearfully and wonderfully made. Wonderful are your works; my soul knows it very well.

Psalm 139:14 (ESV)

## HER THOUGHTS

## HER APPLICATION

*You are fearfully and wonderfully made.*

*Today's Date:*

## HER PRAYERS

### Scripture

And blessed is she who believed that there would be a fulfillment of what was spoken to her from the Lord.

Luke 1:45 (ESV)

## HER THOUGHTS

## HER APPLICATION

*Believe that God will fufill what He spoke.*

*Today's Date:*

## HER PRAYERS

### Scripture

Then Jesus answered her, "O woman, great is your faith! Be it done for you as you desire." And her daughter was healed instantly.

— Matthew 15:28 (ESV)

## HER THOUGHTS

## HER APPLICATION

*Have great faith!*

*Today's Date:*

## HER PRAYERS

### Scripture

I can do all things through him who strengthens me.
Philippians 4:13 (ESV)

## HER THOUGHTS

## HER APPLICATION

*God shall strengthen you.*

*Today's Date:*

## HER PRAYERS

## Scripture

Trust in the Lord with all your heart, and do not lean on your own understanding.

Proverbs 3:5 (ESV)

## HER THOUGHTS

## HER APPLICATION

*Trust in the Lord!*

*Today's Date:*

## HER PRAYERS

### Scripture

Be still, and know that I am God. I will be exalted among the nations, I will be exalted in the earth!

Psalm 46:10 (ESV)

## HER THOUGHTS

## HER APPLICATION

*Know that He is God!*

*Today's Date:*

## HER PRAYERS

## Scripture

The apostles said to the Lord, "Increase our faith!"
Luke 17:5 (ESV)

## HER THOUGHTS

## HER APPLICATION

*Ask God to increase your faith!*

*Today's Date:*

## HER PRAYERS

### Scripture

For you did not receive the spirit of slavery to fall back into fear, but you have received the Spirit of adoption as sons, by whom we cry, "Abba! Father!"
Romans 8:15 (ESV)

## HER THOUGHTS

## HER APPLICATION

*Rest in your Father's love.*

*My* FAITH *will* MOVE *this* MOUNTAIN!

# A PRAYER FOR FAITH

Dear God,

When my faith has been shakened remind me that faith the size of a mustard seed is more than enough to move a mountain. As I face mountains of anxiety, stress and depression, remind me that I have the authority to command these mountains to move.

Reveal the path that You have laid out before me. I know that it will lead me directly to You. Let Your light continue to shine upon me. Build my faith. Help my unbelief.

Amen.

Today's Date:

## HER PRAYERS

### Scripture

On the day I called, you answered me; my strength of soul you increased.

Psalm 138:3 (ESV)

## HER THOUGHTS

## HER APPLICATION

*Your God will answer when you call!*

*Today's Date:*

## HER PRAYERS

### Scripture

Strength and dignity are her clothing, and she laughs at the time to come.

Proverbs 31:25 (ESV)

## HER THOUGHTS

## HER APPLICATION

*Do not fear the future!*

Today's Date:

## HER PRAYERS

### Scripture

She opens her mouth with wisdom, and the teaching of kindness is on her tongue.
Proverbs 31:26 (ESV)

## HER THOUGHTS

## HER APPLICATION

*Remain kind even as you fight.*

*Today's Date:*

## HER PRAYERS

## Scripture

But when you ask, you must believe and not doubt, because the one who doubts is like a wave of the sea, blown and tossed by the wind.

James 1:6 (ESV)

## HER THOUGHTS

## HER APPLICATION

*Believe without doubt!*

*Today's Date:*

## HER PRAYERS

### Scripture

Then Jesus declared, "I am the bread of life. Whoever comes to me will never go hungry, and whoever believes in me will never be thirsty."

John 6:35 (ESV)

## HER THOUGHTS

## HER APPLICATION

*The Lord will fulfill your every need.*

*Today's Date:*

## HER PRAYERS

### Scripture

They replied, "Believe in the Lord Jesus, and you will be saved—you and your household."

Acts 16:31 (ESV)

## HER THOUGHTS

## HER APPLICATION

*Your faith will bless your whole house.*

*Today's Date:*

## HER PRAYERS

### Scripture

In peace I will lie down and sleep, for you alone, LORD, make me dwell in safety.

Psalm 4:8 (ESV)

## HER THOUGHTS

## HER APPLICATION

*Dwell in the safety of the Lord.*

*Today's Date:*

## HER PRAYERS

### Scripture

I will give thanks to the LORD with my whole heart; I will recount all of your wonderful deeds.

Psalms 9:1 (ESV)

## HER THOUGHTS

## HER APPLICATION

*Give thanks unto the Lord!*

*Today's Date:*

## HER PRAYERS

## Scripture

You make known to me the path of life; you will fill me with joy in your presence, with eternal pleasures at your right hand.

Psalm 16:11 (ESV)

## HER THOUGHTS

## HER APPLICATION

*There are joy and eternal pleasures in his presence.*

*Today's Date:*

## HER PRAYERS

### Scripture

May he give you the desire of your heart and make all your plans succeed.

Psalm 20:4 (ESV)

## HER THOUGHTS

## HER APPLICATION

*Your plans will succeed!*

# GOD REFRESHES

*my soul.*

# A PRAYER FOR JOY

Heavenly Father,

You are the joy of my strength. Consume my heart and mind with the joy of your love. Help me to remain joyful, even in times of trouble. Refresh my soul. Save me from the troubles that threaten to consume my mind. Help me to laugh in the face of tribulation. Remind me of Your strength and Your promises. Allow them to be the safeguards of my joy.

Amen.

Today's Date:

## HER PRAYERS

### Scripture

The LORD gives strength to his people; the LORD blesses his people with peace.

Psalm 29:11 (ESV)

### HER THOUGHTS

### HER APPLICATION

*May God bless you with strength and peace.*

*Today's Date:*

## HER PRAYERS

## Scripture

Cast your cares on the LORD and he will sustain you; he will never let the righteous be shaken.

Psalm 55:22 (ESV)

## HER THOUGHTS

## HER APPLICATION

*God won't let you be shaken!*

*Today's Date:*

## HER PRAYERS

## Scripture

She dresses herself with strength and makes her arms strong.

Proverbs 31:17 (ESV)

## HER THOUGHTS

## HER APPLICATION

*Dress yourself in God's strength!*

*Today's Date:*

## HER PRAYERS

### Scripture

Your word is a lamp for my feet, a light on my path.
Psalm 119:105 (ESV)

## HER THOUGHTS

## HER APPLICATION

*God will direct your path.*

*Today's Date:*

## HER PRAYERS

### Scripture

When I consider your heavens, the work of your fingers, the moon and the stars, which you have set in place, what is mankind that you are mindful of them, human beings that you care for them?

Psalm 8:3-4 (ESV)

## HER THOUGHTS

## HER APPLICATION

*You serve a marvelous God!*

Today's Date:

## HER PRAYERS

### Scripture

Even though I walk through the darkest valley, I will fear no evil, for you are with me; your rod and your staff, they comfort me.

Psalm 23:4 (ESV)

## HER THOUGHTS

## HER APPLICATION

*He will be with you and comfort you.*

*Today's Date:*

## HER PRAYERS

### Scripture

As Scripture says, "Anyone who believes in him will never be put to shame."
Romans 10:11 (ESV)

## HER THOUGHTS

## HER APPLICATION

*You won't be put to shame!*

*Today's Date:*

## HER PRAYERS

### Scripture

He will not let your foot slip—
he who watches over you will
not slumber.

Psalm 121:3 (ESV)

## HER THOUGHTS

## HER APPLICATION

*He is always watching over you.*

*Today's Date:*

## HER PRAYERS

### Scripture

We are afflicted in every way, but not crushed; perplexed, but not driven to despair.
2 Corinthians 4:8 (ESV)

## HER THOUGHTS

## HER APPLICATION

*We will not be crushed.*

Today's Date:

## HER PRAYERS

### Scripture

Jesus summoned His twelve disciples and gave them authority over unclean spirits, to cast them out, and to heal every disease and every sickness.

Matthew 10:1 (NASV)

## HER THOUGHTS

## HER APPLICATION

*He has given us authority.*

# Author's Acknowledgements

First and foremost, I give all glory to God. I am nothing without Him. In the process of breast cancer and writing this book, the word of God got me through. God gave me the power to believe in my passion and pursue my dreams. I could never have done this without the faith I have in the Almighty.

To my parents Christine and Samuel Melton, Sr.: THANK YOU for everything. There is no way I could've gone through this journey without you two being by my side, praying for me daily, and, most of all, encouraging me through my weakest moments. I can barely find the words to express my gratitude for all the wisdom, love, and support you two have given me. You guys are my #1 fans and for that I am eternally grateful. If I am blessed to live long enough, I hope I will be as good a parent to my children as you two are and always have been to me. I love you, Mom and Dad.

To my husband, Derrick Dotson: What can I say? You were my lifeline! I am so thankful that I had you in my corner, pushing me when I was ready to give up. Thank you for lying in bed with me days at a time just to be close to me. You are my forever love and my hero! Thanks for not just believing, but knowing that I could do this! I love you, always & forever!

To Danita Brown and Linda Wesby: How could I have done this without the two of you? I couldn't. Thank you for making me laugh when I was in tears. Thank you for speaking life into me when I felt that it was slipping away. Thank you for standing in the gap as a mom when my mom couldn't be present. Thank you for loving me as if I were your own. Words could never express how much you both mean to me.

To my phenomenal tribe: Kimberly Melton, Sissiretta Owens, Cassandra Johnson, Gabriel Sehar, Andrea Nawls, Rose Flowers, Tracy Gallagher, Paula Bingham, Tasha Renee McGregory, Regina Miller, Tonza Taylor, Malcolm Hunt, LaToya Archibald, Reshonn Saul, Tracey Sturdivant, Angela Maxwell, and Nadya Carlisle.

I love you all! Thank you for always showing up for me!

## Stay Connected

Thank you for using *A Fighter's Journey: Journal and Devotional.* LaToya looks forward to connecting with you. Here are a few ways you can connect with the author and stay updated on new releases, speaking engagements, products, and more.

| | |
|---|---|
| FACEBOOK | Pink Savvy, INC. |
| INSTAGRAM | @pinksavvyinc |
| WEBSITE | www.pinksavvyinc.org |
| EMAIL | info@pinksavvyinc.org |

www.ingramcontent.com/pod-product-compliance
Lightning Source LLC
Chambersburg PA
CBHW041232240426
43673CB00010B/318